HILLBILLY DRUG BABY : THE POEMS

Book 1 of the Hillbilly Drug Baby series

DISCARD

JESSE-RAY LEWIS

Virginia

These poems are written from the author's experience and perspective.

Published in the United States by WriteLife Publishing
(An imprint of Boutique of Quality Books Publishing Company, Inc.)
www.writelife.com

978-1-60808-193-6 (p)
978-1-60808-194-3 (e)

Library of Congress Control Number: 2018930813

First editor: Andrea Brunais
Second editor: Pearlie Tan
Book and cover design by Robin Krauss, www.bookformatters.com
Cover photograph by Hal Gibson

Praise for *Hillbilly Drug Baby: The Poems*

"Raw and righteous, with indignant courage and an original voice, Jesse-Ray Lewis somehow poeticizes the brutal, all-too relevant struggle of a prodigal son in Appalachia. His work is uniquely framed by the horrifying, inspiring biography of a nobody with plenty to say. *Hillbilly Drug Baby: The Poems* is a dispatch from darkest America you won't soon forget."

—Ran Henry,
Author of the definitive biography *Spurrier:
How the Ball Coach Taught the South to Play Football*

"I come from a cave of broken hearts" is only one line from *Hillbilly Drug Baby: The Poems*, but it reveals much of what is to be found in this book of poetry. From raw pain to poignant reflection, poet Jesse-Ray Lewis plumbs the depths of despair with his words. Drawing them with a pen dipped in his own life's blood, he reveals glimmers of light and hope in the darkest of places. Lewis's journey from drug baby to user, to becoming a dealer, and finally, a seeker, is cast without apology in strong language. Some will find it difficult to read; it is from life. Unafraid, he probes our deepest fears; What would it be like to live that life? To plumb the depths of hell? To find an earthly savior loving yet stern and one who probes the crusty exterior, digging deep to find the gentle heart which lies beneath?

—Saundra Kelley,
Author of *Southern Appalachian Storytellers: Interviews
with Sixteen Keepers of the Oral Tradition* and *The Day the
Mirror Cried*, a prizewinning collection of stories and poems

Upcoming Books in
the Hillbilly Drug Baby Series

Table of Contents

Meth Baby, Crack Baby

The first time my first foster mother
smacked the shit out of me
was at the hospital
when I said
to the woman at the desk
fat and blonde
who didn't seem to want to move her ass
for a kid like me,
"Fuck you. Do it!"

Of course it hurt!
My foster mother pimp-slapped me.
Back of her fingers to the back of my head.
I was twelve, maybe thirteen.
We weren't at the hospital for me.
We were there for her son.
He worked there.
We had dropped him off.

Then my foster mother remembered
she needed my birth records
to enroll me in school, maybe.
I needed something, too.
I needed to talk to the dude who grabbed me
by the legs and pulled me out

when my mother gave birth.
Blonde fat-ass went to the back
to look him up.
Foster mother parked in the hallway
while I went up in an elevator.
Inside an office
the dude didn't say a word.
He showed me the paper, my mother's blood test.
I kinda ripped it out of his hands.
I saw everything I already knew.

It was a *list*.
How many drugs was she on?
Two stood out to me. Meth and coke.
For me, a baby not yet born.

I looked at the words. Meth and coke.
I couldn't say what I felt.
Meth and coke.
Empty. Not really feeling anything
but feeling something.
Numb.
I know what they say about crack babies.
I'm not angry at her.
I've done those drugs myself.

I looked at the paper like you would glance
at a piece of junk mail.
It wasn't something that needed to be proven.
It's not like I didn't already know.
They'd told me all my life.

Jesse-Ray Lewis

When they went to my father
to see if he wanted to raise his twelve-year-old son
he couldn't pass the simple test
of not having needles strewn all over the floor.
He told me about my drug-mother
but he also told me so much bullshit
I had to find out myself.

Everyone always asked me
about my mom.
My missing mom.
And now I knew.
I'd seen it.

They tried to get me to talk about it;
the doctors and counselors when I was in foster care.
It's hard to pay attention to what people say
when you're stoned out of your mind
on painkillers and weed.

I laugh, remembering
how even in sixth grade I was so fuckin' high
that mothers pointed me out
to their children
and told them not to be like me.

I drank, too,
told that foster family I wanted to get away from them.
But what I really wanted was dirt.
I meant six feet down in the dirt.
I meant death.

In those days
did I think about tonight
tomorrow, next week?
Try the next minute.
I never thought about the future
until I was sixteen
when my meth-dealer-father-figure
gave me my first job and
taught me to deal drugs and to plan.

"Live in the moment
but always think about the future," he said.
"If you don't think about the future
you're fucked."

And finally,
after I thought about the future
I walked away.

I still think about my
meth-dealer-father-figure
and I still use the word father
to describe him. But I couldn't stay in that life.
No more gang, no more meth
no more deal drops.
I got tired
of intimidating people.

Now I'm headed, maybe, to college.
To a job. To working toward a place of my own.
To living with my girl.

Jesse-Ray Lewis

Hillbilly drug baby? Maybe that's who I came out as.
But it's not who I want to be.

If people call me a crack baby, I could give a shit.
That's not who I am.

Who do I want to be?
I'm still trying to figure that out.
A positive role model?
I like those words.

But can I change?
I can't seem to find who I am.

At my twelve-step meetings
they want me to surrender.
Maybe tomorrow or next week.
But not this minute.

Seven and Seven

Born with the dope already in me
when I came out, they put in needles
to get me off the shit.

It didn't work.

I remember being
on the playground
thinking, damn
if I jumped off this slide
I could go home
sneak into my dad's room
and take some of them candies
that made me feel silly.

Once, I ate seven and felt like
I was going to heaven.
I was seven years old.

Didn't know what they were
until my dad caught me
and taught me how to snort them properly.

Comfort Food

Growing up
I mostly ate noodles
I fixed myself.
I don't remember anyone
ever cooking for me.
Except my favorite meal
"bitter potatoes."

Potatoes mixed with
Xanax.
First eaten when I was three.

That I don't remember.
But this I know:
I liked them even better
when I got older.

Home Fights

Fights with my dad
would start over nothing
or anything.

I'd ask him, "Why are you so dickish?"
"Cuz."
"Well, fuck you."
"Fuck you!"

Then we would fight.
It would end when
one of us was on the ground
and couldn't get up.

There were times when
I thought he'd killed me
or I'd killed him.

How did I know I was the one killed?
I'd wake up three days later.

After the final foster family,
after I couch-hopped
to a friend whose boyfriend
threw me out after a month,

I went to my aunt.
She called my Dad
and dumped me on him
when I didn't ask for that.

I ended up in that hellhole trailer
with him
and his bitchy-ass girlfriend
and my uncle.

When the landlord said I couldn't live there
my Dad told me,
"Call somebody who cares."
I asked him, "Hey, you know anyone
who has a couch I could crash on?"
He said, "No, fuck you."

So I left. Again.
In and out of that trailer
over the years.
Bounced around
from my Dad to my grandma to
my aunts to foster families.

Why did I go back?
Because he's my dad
and I didn't have anything else.

Irony of Childhood

I sold drugs to my dad
thinking, *I'm making money!*
But later
I found out he was paying me
with money he got from the government
to take care of me.

Running in Place

My Dad
drinks till he runs away
from everything.
Can't blame him though.
I've done it too.
Torn down the walls
with the smoldering smoke of an addict.

My memories are fuzzy pictures.
I'm trying to fight him, but he's
the person I would love to be.
With no responsibilities.

I want to run away from thoughts.

I'm a clone of him
which makes me want
to puke blood.

Pain

Curse this lost, broken life.
I need someone
but I push them away.

Inside I'm screaming.

Am I on the edge of death?
I'm in the freezing rain.

Five million life tests and
I've failed all of them.

Thousands of fragments of thoughts
like dead weight on my back.

My throat tightens
like a punch in the chest.

I am a flower
roasting in the sun.
Wilting.

I am tied to a tree.
Hanging.
Swinging.

Torment

Stressed
I put on a bulletproof vest
'bout to go crazy
on those dumb motherfucking babies.

I'm done with the bullshit.
I'm going back to being an asshole.
A fucking savage
with no regrets.

Trying to vent the fumes of chemicals
that would burn
someone's retinas out
to make them see the darkness I see.

Two knees on the ground.
screaming
"PLEASE! MAN! PLEASE!"

His pleas mean nothing to me.
I feed on them.
I love to hear the scream
dream of the pain I've experienced
try to get rid of it through him
as he chokes on puke and blood

and drowns
to death.
His body shudders.

Danger is a bloodstained grin
on the face
of a person who never gives in.

Mental War

I cry inside.
I ask why
disaster strikes.

I get in a fight
not physical—
but a mental war.
Defeated
like a statistic on a board.

Who cares? A board chairman who doesn't
give a fuck about me
or any city, town, or even the kids
who try to get by
with a scrap of food?

Stuck in a revolution, spinning
drowning in emotion.
I want to turn the broken dial of my life back
to the same high
most guys hide from
staying up two months straight
hallucinating till my brain is mush.

I'd push my mind to keep going
even if these shadow people kept following me
down an empty street
headlights in the distance.

Drugs
ease their minds from rape.
Drugs
get them beat to a bloody pulp.

Let the bombs come.
We doomed ourselves anyway.
Just grab a couple nines
get your mind straight.

In my mind
the war started
long ago.

Just be ready
for the moment
when you shoot a person
and you turn them over
and it's there:
your face.

Zach

When I asked my father about my real mother
he said he met her in a brothel and forgot to pull out.
It might be true.
My cousin Zach was a Mistake, too.
That's what Zach told me they called him.
A Mistake.
He was three years older than me.
The first time I met him, he was shooting up.

Zach is dead now.
He always wanted to die.
He would roll his clothes in dirt
and take them in the house
so he could smell like death.

His parents told him he was a Mistake.

He stayed fucked up on drugs, mostly
because of what his life was like.
He was the only person I talked to.

Zach's dad let him leave the house
so Zach would tell me things.
Zach knew things I didn't know.

My dad wouldn't let me leave the house.

Zach died a long time ago.
He was only thirteen.
He was all doped up.
There was a fire. He didn't make it out.

Zach didn't make it out of that burning house.
But I made it out of that life.

Portrait of Two Fathers

To know about my fathers
first, you need to know what
a trap house is.

A trap house is
where you go if you want to sell drugs
or get drugs
or do drugs.

When my aunt had had enough of me
my father could have said to the state,
"You're not taking my son."

But he got into some substances
that made him not care.
My dad just did not care.

In his trap house, there were needles on the floor
tire tracks in the driveway
and boot tracks at the front door
from all the buying and selling
from all the coming and going.

It was easy for the police to catch him.
Straight easy.
We had tire marks from our driveway
to the street.

My meth-dealer-father-figure
taught me the drug trade.
He was careful.
Everything was tight and clean.
There were only three pieces
of furniture in his trap houses:
two plastic chairs
and a plastic table.

He talked to me. He listened.
He taught me things.
He knew everything about me.

He could see when I was getting mad.
Ten seconds before I snapped
I would flick my tongue along
my lower teeth.
He called it "lickin' angry."

He knew I was tired of going nowhere.
He blessed me out, which means
he gave me permission to leave.
This intimidating man who
could make the devil weep.

Hal Doesn't Want Me To Say Muh-Fuckah

I'm working on my language.
This is harder than it sounds.
Sometimes I'm about to say
what Hal calls "curse words"
and I stop.

If it wasn't for Hal, I'd be dead.
He doesn't want me to use bad language.

According to my grandma
my first word was "dad."
My second word was "fuck."
I was a toddler, I guess.
I dropped something.
And I was like, "fuck."

My grandma never said much.
She cried instead
because of what her life was like.
She only talked when we were alone
but that almost never happened.
There were always people around.

I don't remember an adult in the house
who wasn't fucked up on drugs
except a Child Protective Services worker.
Once.

What did my grandma say to me?
She said, "Even your family
can fuck you in the ass and never give you a reach-
around."
I don't know why I laugh when I remember that.
My grandma was like my mother.
I called her Mom.

She never told me how she felt about being raped.

We slept on a mattress on the floor.
We couldn't afford anything else for some fuckin'
reason.
When it was cold, my grandma told me to imagine
we were in the Little House on the Prairie
and to cover up.
I didn't know what that was
but I would get all warm.
Once in a while
she would sing to me.

The things I saw.

I saw a man's punishment.
He owed a debt of drugs and money
to the wrong people.
I saw rape.
I saw meth.

I saw a girl get hit in the neck with a needle
for making her boyfriend mad.
I saw her face turn from angry
to freaking the fuck out.
I saw people I can't name
do things I can't describe
to make other people hurt.

So when I say muh-fuckah
I know what a muh-fuckah is.

But Hal is trying to save my life
and I want my life to be saved.
So I try not to say muh-fuckah.

Hal's the only person who ever said to me,
"I'm proud of you."

When he said that
the thought that came into my head was,
"I'm going to fuck that up."

Muh-fuckah. I try to explain the word to Hal.
A muh-fuckah can be an asshole.
Or muh-fuckah can be a noun.
If you just walk by it,
it's a word you use when
you don't know somebody's name
and you have to call them something.

Hal's right. Language is important.
But because the world is fucked up
cleaning up my language is harder than you think.

I could stop saying the word "muh-fuckah"
but if I look around
and all I see
is a world full of muh-fuckahs
does anything really change?

If you took the word "fuck" out of my world, what
would I like to see?
I would like to describe that world in a way that meant
"good."
I know everybody can't get along
but I'd like a word in the English language that meant
"OK."

Like you're dealing with it
and you can get past it.
If such a word existed
I might see the point of making the effort.
But cleaning up my language is harder than you know.

I want to read this at a poetry slam
and at the end, say,
"Thank you, muh-fuckahs!"
And have them know just what I mean.

Demons

A demon
scheming
took my bloodstained heart.
Smoke rises
when people die.

I am screaming
fighting crawling
naked
on broken glass.

My girlfriend
fights her demons.
I cradle mine.
Try to hide
but there's no hiding.

On forms
they ask for next-of-kin
but I have none.

The Casket

I find a single droplet of hope
and choke on it.

Acidic visions from when I was in prison
find me sinking into a hole.

Fuck this coffin!
I'm rippin' it out of the ground
with a smile
blood pressure dialed up.

Concealed within is a vial
of blood mixed with tears
my fears come true:
The casket drowns in gasoline
and is lit.

Isn't it sad?
Seeing the burnt wood of it?

The demon I've concealed
creeps out on burned hands and feet.

The casket starts to break.
Shatters, falls, makes a dent
in the part of my mind that's still sane.

Now the demon controls me
consoles me
feels the pain with me.
Now I walk this dream of chaos
falling into a sparkling vat;
a trap.

Scream at myself to stop
but I'm inside the maggot-infested
burning-flesh-smelling cesspit.

JUST QUIT! I tell myself.
Deal with these things.
Without drugs, without needles
without even poems and pens.

I jump in headfirst.
Seconds remain for the melting brain
to still maintain. I grab the edge
but I'm sliding down deeper
as my heart
falls, too.

Done, but still
holding
on.

Blue

I don't know why
I've always hated blue.

My grandma said I did
even when I was little.

When I was seven
a kid gave me a blue popsicle.
I tried to
shove it in his eye.

Later when I saw my homies die
they died at the hands
of a gang wearing blue.

Blood

Blood is everything.
Blood is evidence.

Blood is also
my connection to my homies.

In a gang
you "blood in" and you "blood out."

It starts with a beating.
My initiation
was a beating.

It proved my loyalty.
I'm still loyal.

Their blood is my blood.
Stronger than the blood
of my blood relatives.

The only way out of a gang
is to die
or to be "blessed out."

Seven men blessed me out.

The favorite saying
of my meth-dealer-father-figure was
"A speck of blood
can change your whole world."

Blood is evidence.

I still hold
his unbreakable trust.

Death of a Loved One

My grandma was the only mother
I knew.
I called her Mom.
Or Momma.

She never said much.
Mostly she cried.
But when we were alone
sometimes she talked to me.

She was the only one
who took care of me.

I found her.

I walked through the tiny doorway
to the kitchen.

Nothing in it but a black mini-fridge
and beyond it, the living room
with a mattress on the floor and an old box TV.

She lay on the floor
only hours after she said
something I will never forget.

We had had some stupid argument
and she had said
I would give her a heart attack.

I held her for hours.
There was foam at her mouth
and blood as I cradled her.

I am the one who closed her eyes.

I remember when the paramedics
took her away from me,
this woman who cared for me.

Together we lived with my father's violence.
We slept together
on that mattress
on the floor.

No more. But I still wake up
thinking I am hugging Momma.

I have nightmare
memories.
They eat me alive.

Do people know what it's like
to see your dead loved ones
in front of you?

I wish I could talk to her
but she just sits there
and stares into my soul.

Jesse-Ray Lewis

I didn't cry then
but now
I scream,
Why did you have to OD?

I've got a place now.
A house with a roof
where I am safe.

Please.
I'm sorry.
I miss you.
I'm honestly afraid
of what my future holds.

I hope
I can live in it
and not want to die
every minute.

A Good Man

I never thought I was a good man.
I never thought love was significant.
Then I met a girl.

I have found a new feeling:
Love.
Even drugs never made
lonely thoughts disappear.

Love is confusing
and the best feeling.
I've never felt so good.

She cares and she dares me
to have thoughts of a higher being.
I am like a baby with new teeth coming in.

Love is feeling flooded
like a turkey being basted.
I write in a new voice
that is tender but firm.

Once I lived in a heap of lies
death and drugs.
I had a gun
(part of that life).
I was going to end my life.

Now I love fresh air
like the breath of the girl I love
who's not here but I wish she was here.

Now I can feel things
like a hug
like the belief that I deserve to live
like the feeling of new teeth coming in.

First Love

Because I love you.
Because I'm broken and you put me back together.
Because I have never been honest with myself
        until now.

I'm weird and crazy and
you put me in a
        FEELING!

I die in my mind every minute
without you.

Anticipation from Another State

I hope when I see you, you don't freeze.
Please someone get me to her.

I want to fast forward a couple of years
my tears of sadness and depression gone.

From stressful
to successful.

Please someone get me to her.

Pondering the thought
of being taught nothing
that I had no reason for living.

But from a new height, I learned
to fight for what I want.

Writing a rhyme to last.
Now's the time for us.

Purple

The most beautiful purple flowers
lay on my chest
in the casket.
Just a trigger pull away.

Once, twice,
maybe three times
I almost—
I had a gun, you know.

When I look out
(no drugs now)
where people see snow falling
I still see blood pouring
mixed with unspeakable things.

My tortured life is full of
gore-filled memories.
I see eyes gouged out and replaced with needles,
a mouth cut open
with a pipe placed inside.

Sometimes I wish
the blood was from
a dead fetus.
Me.

So that I never would have been
born of a mother
who only cared about
the next high.

I don't wonder about her at all.
How her life has been.

Instead, I thank the girl who gave me hope.

She stitches the wounds of loneliness
and addiction.
I just want to hold her,
my happiness.

I will fight to reach the light.
I have changed my life.
I feel like my heart
has finally
been treated
with tenderness.

Happy

The happiest I've ever been
was the week that my girl said
"I love you"
after I thought she would
never talk to me again.

She wanted nothing to do with me.
(The drugs.)

A happy memory before that?
I have none.
I have always been numb
ever since I can remember.

Where I'm from
you are never a kid.
They told me that
if you can walk and talk
you're not a kid.

Kids shouldn't be able to hear things
like my grandma saying
she was raped as a child.

The only time I ever
looked at the sky and thought
this is beautiful
was the first time I did acid.
I walked outside and everything was vibrant.

Like *Holy Shit!*
The world was awesome
and colors melted into other colors.

Utterances from the Present

Mad is a word I know too well.
I think everyone is mad at me
or I'm mad in the sense
of insanity.

People with no needle tracks say they know
what rock bottom is.
Do they know what it's like to sleep abandoned
by everyone
but surrounded by everyone?

I slept in a house whose foundation was vile
on a ground made of maggots and the spit of the
vengeful.

They spit on the grave of a lost boy.

Utterances from the past:

I live in darkness.
I hear the night cries of a man with no fight left in him.
The only thing left is hollowed out
and emblazoned with the mark of addict
an imprint on my skull.

Mad is a word I know too well.
The world is filled with interruptions
from reality.

I never knew love could surround me.
I only knew the bondage
of murderous straps of barbed wire.

I walk out of the old life into a paradise without lies.
I confess my thoughts to something or someone
that won't judge.
Light as a feather.

And for the future me
utterances from the present:

Don't fuck anything up.
Have compassion and courage.
Get through
every fence you built
to keep your dreams at bay.

Jail, Spring 2017

I wake up in a cell
where I've come to face
two charges:
possession and being a fugitive,
missing two court dates.

I wake up from a dream, crying
though I know not to cry in jail
in front of men.
My father would beat me unconscious
for crying.

I've broken the cardinal rule.
I've turned myself in.
In the drug trade
you don't get caught
and you don't turn yourself in.

I cry because the man
who's helped me might not
be there when I get out.
Afraid I'll forget his number
I carve it into my arm with sharp metal.
Hal, with his
Safe House.

A big dude
with huge biceps
pushes me around
calls me names.
I let him, for two days.

Then I tell him my street name.
He lifts up his shirt
and shows me his Aryan Nation tattoos
to prove the man he is.
He *apologizes*. Word spreads.

They all know my street name.
The fifty guys in the pod
know what I'm capable of.
After that, they don't bother me.

There's a concrete bench to sit on
with three guys watching TV
laughing.
I force another guy, a child beater
to give me his lunches.

I hate slipping
back into the power
of violence
where everything changes
and I am untouchable again.

The judge says
"You're released"
but the paperwork doesn't catch up
and I'm stuck for three more days
with men in a pod stinking of soap.

Jesse-Ray Lewis

A man I know, maybe fifty years old
with a bad case of meth mouth, says
"I'm a Jesus freak"
and offers me meth.
It's on him, right there in jail.

That's the etiquette.
If you say you've got some
then you have to line it out.
I tell him, "No, man. Not now."
But I want it so bad I can't tell you.

I wasn't about to tell him I was clean
and sober.
Done with that life.

If they didn't let me out of jail
I'd lose everything I'd worked for:
Ninety days of being clean
and not sleeping outside
in a scratched-out hole under a tree.

And then I'm out
and for days
when I talk to people
I hold one wrist
crossed over the other, as if
the cuffs are still on.

Trust

I hope I can get there.
Where, I'm not sure.
I have no plan
except to stay off drugs.

Part of me wants to trust
but I was raped.
I haven't told many people
I have nightmares.

I'm used to having to worry.
If I didn't worry
something really bad would happen.
I would starve
or die.

I want to be the kid I never got to be.
I want to see things in the soft bright
light of the future.

Origins

If I die
that would only pass my hurt
to someone else.

My old way of life
is disappearing.

Misunderstood.

I was a kid.
Not from the hood
but from tears
filled with blood and money.

I come from a cave of broken hearts.

Regrets

Everything I did.
Was it worth it?

I'm trapped behind a wall
of ice so thick
you can't scream through it.

I think of my dead best friend.
His eyes rolled back.
I try to remember his life.

I came close to Death
who I know as a friend.
A lover of sorts
one that a bullet could summon.

Doesn't Add Up

I keep going back
to square one.
Daring to go further.

With
two check stubs
four debts
and a fucked-up mind to maintain.

Indecision

Two years ago
I told myself
if I ran away from the trauma
I'd be fine.

It would go away
forever.

I never
faced the flashbacks
clean and sober.
Only by getting high.

The demons tell me
to give up.

A fog settles
between me
and my goals.

I just want to live
away
in the woods again.

Depression

I go to work thinking
I can make it through the day.
Try to do the things I'm told.

I've been sober for five months.
My mind tells me:
If you just slip back
you will be fine.
I dose myself
to make myself feel better.

I fall deeper.

I had a career as a dealer.
Now I'm the fiend
trying to get a hit.

I don't need it.
I seek it.

I've done everything I can
to make the flashbacks go away.

I wake up with my hands full:
A cup of purple in one
and a pipe in the other.

forgive Me

Today was rough
memories.
My mind is laced with hallucinogens.
Not much of a Higher Being.

Burning senses
and a constant frown
of thoughts
buried.

I try to hide.
They come to me
in dreams.

I'm not looking for pity
but inner divinity.

Are we
human beings
(a not-so-perfect
bundle of atoms)
trying to fuck over everything?

I go
from watching bodies decay
to trying to pray
not to a god
but a form of my worst fears,
my every tear.

I'm stuck in thoughts.
They slowly crawl out
of my Play-Doh-like
brain.
A burnt carcass.
Maybe I'm not insane.

There's been a drought
without light.
I fight to reach the light.

I have abandonment issues.
I have a quick temper.
I have a drug addiction.
I'm scared of the future.
I ask too many questions.

How do I change into something
that I don't know yet?

I burn my thoughts away in smoke
that numbs.

My heart is drifting in an unrelenting tide
of fear of abandonment
and love.

Jesse-Ray Lewis

I can't wait to have thoughts
without fear, hate, anger, sadness.
I hope someone will forgive me.

Walking

I walked out of foster care
when I turned eighteen.
The social worker
was on the way to deliver me
to a homeless shelter.

No way was that happening.

For two months, I worked for my dad's employer.
He didn't pay me.
My payment was being allowed
to live with my hellhole dad in a shitty trailer
in the middle of nowhere
with his bitchy-ass alcoholic girlfriend
who sat around drinking all day.

No way was that going to go on forever.

With the last of my money, maybe thirty dollars
I took a bus to Bluefield.
I got off at Walmart
walked down the road
found a tree to sleep under
and became the richest homeless man in Bluefield.

Hillbilly Drug Baby: The Poems

First panhandling
then turning sixty dollars into drugs
then flipping drugs for more drugs.

Soon I had enough to flip and sell
and do the drugs myself.

Simple Drug Dealer Math, I called it.

People in the apartments
were coming to homeless me
to sell them four thousand dollars
worth of weed that I traded in
at a time.

And then it was over.

I smoked the last bit of my weed
and thought, oh, fuck, I don't feel like
walking four miles
to my supplier
and then walking around town all day
walking and selling.

Walking
walking
walking.
It was the worst part
of being homeless.
Worse than living outside
in winter.

So my final walk
was to Bluefield Union Mission.

Jesse-Ray Lewis

I watched people walking in and out.
There were three doors out front.
I saw which door they used.
I went inside that door.

I said, "Can I have food?
Can I have a place to stay?"
(Where the hell else was I going to get food
and a place to stay?)

To be completely honest
I dealt drugs the first three nights
they put me up
in a motel on the edge
of town.

But I saw something in the faces
of the people inside the mission.
They had lives that
didn't involve
walking miles
every day
and living in abandoned houses
dealing drugs
and being high.

I thought, I want that.
I want to live without walking
from nowhere to nowhere.

Now I walk to and from a Safe House.
I walk to bus stops and the mission and meetings
and even take a walk—just for fun—
up a mountain with a friend.

No more Drug Dealer Money
because that would fuck up everything
I'm trying to do with my life.

I'm not thinking about tomorrow
or next week.
Try the next ten minutes.

For the first time, I have people in my life
I actually want to be like
and I can see myself
walking
into a world
like theirs.

Turning Point

I think of a place:
beautiful green trees
holding onto memories.

Cut my wrists?
Better than reminisce
about being a mental prisoner
tied up with chains.

Bodies on the floor.
Loved ones dead
or comatose
self-inflicted overdose.

Today I'm a young man
trying to pass an entrance exam
breaking up those memories with every word
I write.

I'm stabbing my old life in the back
with a knife made of positives.
I dream of being someone.
I smile.
No one can take away my freedom.
I will not go insane.

I can even sympathize
with those who fed me lies
about how to be a man.

They taught me wrong.
The rainwater made puddles into a reservoir.
Beaten, in cages, controlled by rages.

I struggle.
I will not be a victim.

I fought all my life to survive.
I survived.
Now I'm awake.